Furry Foot Notes

BOOK THREE: Furry Footnotes

©2016 by Leah Wells

Illustrations ©2016 by Naomi Rosenblatt
Photographs ©2016 by Judy Rosenblatt
Cover and book design by Naomi Rosenblatt

HelioTot is an imprint of Heliotrope Books.

All rights reserved. No part of this publication may be reproduced, stored in a retrieval system, or transmitted, in any form or by any means, electronic, mechanical, photocopying, recording, or otherwise, without prior written permission from the publisher: heliotropebooks@gmail.com.

Furry Foot Notes

Leah Wells

Illustrated by Naomi Rosenblatt

HelioTot

New York City

For Emmanuel, Logan, and Penelope

Furry foot notes
in the snow...

Who left them here?
Where did they go?

Four beats to a measure,
the breezes chime.

This forest runs
in four-four time.

First are whole notes,
round and long,

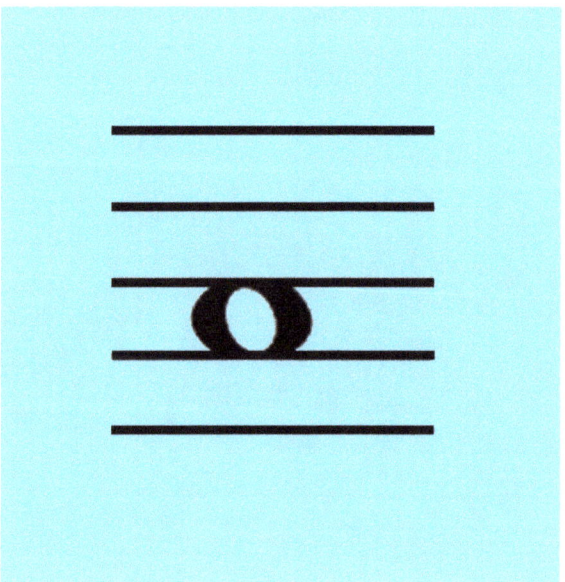

like walking in a slow, slow song.

Half notes are only
half as slow;

their snowy middle tells me so.

Then quarter notes:
one note, one beat,

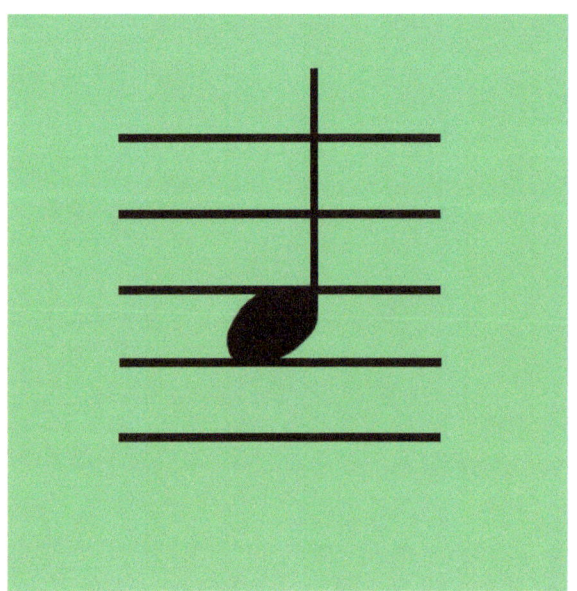

left in the snow by faster feet.

Look...
something that can
dash and flicker...

eighth notes running even quicker!

Sixteenth notes
in a blur
go by,

Like something light
enough to fly.

Furry foot notes in the snow—
Some stop to rest...

...and some just go.

A dotted eighth note
with a flag

=

A bunny, faster than a stag?

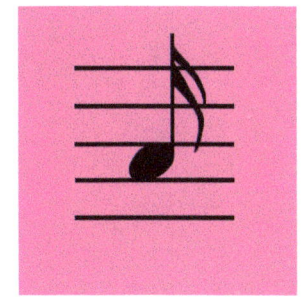  

Around a tree I look by chance

And come upon a forest dance.

A squirrel and raccoon dosey-doeing...

So this is
where they
all were going.

The half notes
with their middles clear

I think were left by
Lady Deer.

The quarter notes—
dog, sheeps...

...and goats?

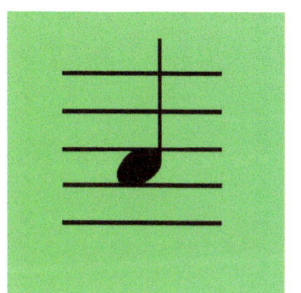

But I can see who left whole notes.

I'm getting kind of scared and so....
I'll run sixteenth notes home....
Allegro!

He's standing up,
I'd better go...

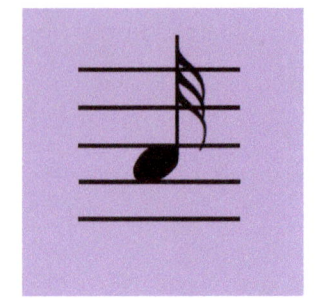

Thirty-second notes now... Presto!

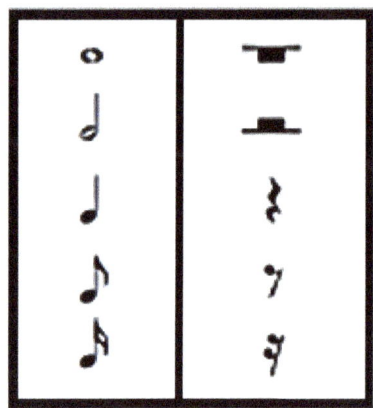

About the Author and Illustrator

They're sisters! They live in New York City.

Leah Wells, to the right, plays stringed instruments – the guitar, banjo, mandolin, and fiddle – and teaches music. She is developing the *How Do You Do Music*™ series to help children read and enjoy music. Her first book, *Games That Sing*, was published in 2011 by Heritage Music Press. Leah is married with two sons.

Naomi Rosenblatt, to the left, is a painter, illustrator, designer, and the founder of Heliotrope Books. Together with her sister she is starting the HelioTot imprint for children.

www.ingramcontent.com/pod-product-compliance
Lightning Source LLC
Chambersburg PA
CBHW041632040426
42446CB00022B/3483